STINGRAYS

PowerKiDS press™

New York

Shane McFee

Published in 2008 by The Rosen Publishing Group, Inc.
29 East 21st Street, New York, NY 10010

First Edition

Editor: Jennifer Way
Book Design: Kate Laczynski
Photo Researcher: Nicole Pristash

Photo Credits: Cover, p. 1 © Shutterstock.com; p. 5 © Bill Curtsinger/Getty Images; pp. 7, 9, 11, 13, 15, 17, 19 © Shutterstock.com; p. 21(main) © Patricia Danna; p. 21 (inset) © Getty Images.

Library of Congress Cataloging-in-Publication Data

McFee, Shane.
  Stingrays / Shane McFee. — 1st ed.
      p. cm. — (Poison!)
  Includes index.
  ISBN-13: 978-1-4042-3797-1 (lib. bdg.)
  ISBN-10: 1-4042-3797-6 (lib. bdg.)
  1. Stingrays—Juvenile literature. I. Title.
  QL638.8.M34 2008
  597.3'5—dc22

                                        2007001476

Manufactured in the United States of America

CONTENTS

STINGRAYS

Have you ever seen a stingray? You may have seen one on the beach. Stingrays have a flat body and a thin tail. Sometimes they are called pancake sharks.

There are at least 200 different **species** of stingrays in the world. Stingrays get their name because they have sharp **stingers**. Their stings can be very painful and even deadly. Do you want to know more about these strange creatures? This book will tell you about the biggest ones and how to escape being stung.

Stingrays live in warm ocean waters all over the world. Some people like to swim with stingrays. There is even a place called Stingray City in the Cayman Islands where you can do just that!

COUSINS OF THE SHARK

Stingrays are a kind of fish called Chondrichthytes. Sharks are also Chondrichthytes. Sharks and stingrays do not have bones. They have **cartilage** instead. Cartilage bends like rubber. This allows stingrays and sharks to move quickly in the water.

Stingrays and sharks breathe through **gills**. These are located inside their gill slits. Gill slits look like slots on the bottom of a stingray's body.

Most stingrays do not have fins. They have large rounded sides that look like wings. When they swim, it looks like they are flying.

The cartilage in a stingray's body bends easily and helps the stingray move through the water quickly.

A SPECIAL SENSE

Stingrays have eyes on the top of their body. Their mouth is on the bottom. This means stingrays cannot always use their eyes to hunt for food. They have a very strong sense of smell.

Stingrays also have special **organs** near their mouth called ampullae of Lorenzini. These organs can sense the **electrical charges** of other fish. This sense is called electrosense. The stingray's ampullae of Lorenzini help it find animals that are hurt or helpless, which it can then eat!

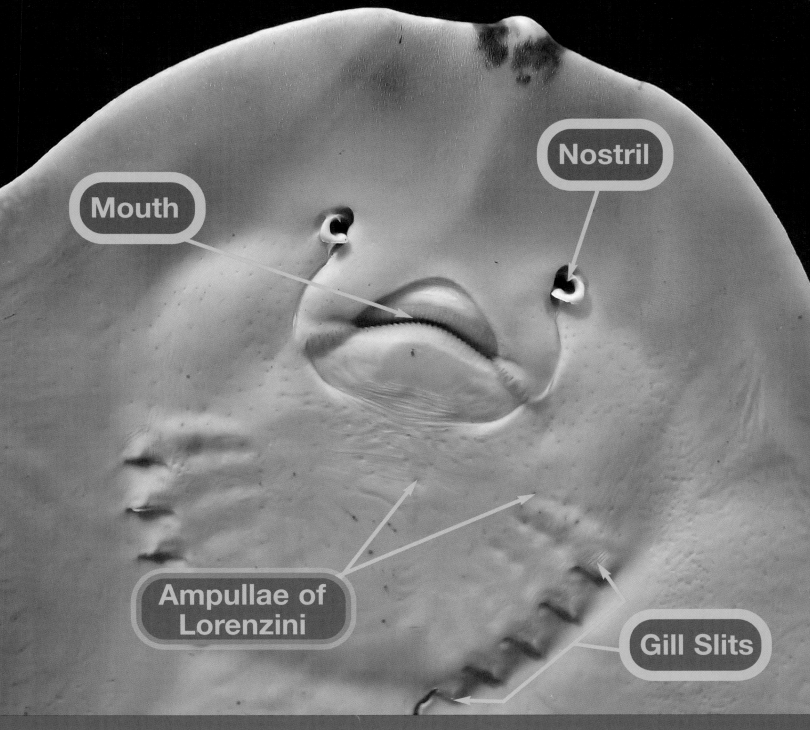

Mouth

Nostril

Ampullae of Lorenzini

Gill Slits

This is the underside of a stingray. You can see its nostrils, mouth, gill slits, and ampullae of Lorenzini. Gill slits are what stingrays use to breathe. The ampullae of Lorenzini are the small dark spots near its mouth.

LIFE ON THE OCEAN FLOOR

Most stingrays live in **tropical** ocean waters. Some species even live in freshwater. Stingrays live on the ocean floor because that is where their **prey** lives. This is why stingrays are called bottom-feeders.

Some stingrays have coloring that **camouflages** them. Their camouflage allows stingrays to mix in with the color of the ocean floor and hide from **predators**. Many stingrays hide by covering themselves in the sand. This makes them a danger to swimmers, who might step on them and get stung.

When they are lying flat on the ocean floor, stingrays can be hard to see. This not only lets them hide from predators but also from animals that stingrays are hunting.

WHAT DO STINGRAYS EAT?

Stingrays are carnivores. This means they live by eating other animals. Stingrays eat smaller fish and crustaceans. Crustaceans are ocean animals that have shells. Crabs, lobsters, and shrimp are crustaceans. Stingrays have very strong teeth, which are able to crush, or break up, shells.

Some stingrays find hidden prey by moving their body. This moves around the sand on the ocean floor. The unlucky animals are uncovered right under the stingray's mouth.

Crabs, like the one shown here, are one of several kinds of crustaceans that stingrays eat. Stingrays are also eaten by sharks and sometimes even by larger stingrays.

OUCH!

Stingrays have very sharp stingers, called **spines**. The spines grow out of the stingrays' tail the way your fingernails grow out of your hand. Sometimes the spines will break off after the stingray uses them to sting. Stingrays can grow new ones.

A stingray's **venom** is strong to keep it safe from predators. Stingrays use their spines only in **defense**. The spine **injects** venom into an animal like a doctor's needle.

Stingray attacks are very uncommon. If a stingray is scared, it will usually swim away. Stingray venom is very painful and dangerous to people.

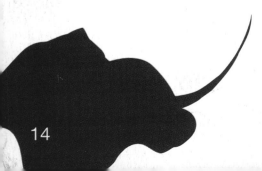

Most stingrays will try to escape when they feel they are in danger. If they cannot get away, they can quickly flip their long tail and give a sting to an enemy.

MATING

Unlike most fish, stingrays do not lay eggs. Females give birth to babies that have grown inside their body.

Stingrays usually **mate** during the winter. The male stingray swims up to the female and bites her to get her attention. Then he floats on top of her to mate with her. Baby stingrays are born about five months later.

Female stingrays usually give birth to a litter of up to 10 babies. The young stingrays usually hide in water that is not deep until they are big enough to live on their own.

The female stingray uses her electrosense to help her draw male stingrays to her for mating. If a female stingray does not wish to mate with the male stingray that comes over, she might sting him!

THE BLUE-SPOTTED RIBBONTAIL

The blue-spotted ribbontail ray is one of the strangest-looking animals in the ocean. Unlike many stingrays, it does not hide with camouflage. It has very colorful blue spots. The rest of its body is usually yellow or brown. The blue-spotted ribbontail ray lives in the ocean near Africa, Japan, and Australia.

This is a very shy stingray. It will sting only if it feels that it is in danger. The stings from this creature are very painful.

The blue-spotted ribbontail stingray is known for the bright blue spots on its body. Divers in the South Pacific Ocean's tropical waters sometimes enjoy a sighting of this shy animal.

THE SHORT-TAIL STINGRAY

Short-tail stingrays are the largest stingrays in the world. They are so big that they are also called bull rays.

Short-tail rays can grow up to 6 feet (2 m) across. They can weigh more than 700 pounds (317.5 kg).

Short-tail rays usually have two stingers. The front one is smaller and does not inject venom. The rear stinger is much larger. These stingrays can move their tail very quickly to sting. The venom of the short-tail ray is powerful, but it is usually not deadly because most people are stung in the foot.

Steve Irwin, the Crocodile Hunter, was killed by an Australian bull ray in 2006. The stinger went through his heart.

Most stingrays sting people in the foot. Inset: *Steve Irwin was stung through the heart by a stingray. This kind of sting is uncommon.*

WHAT SHOULD YOU DO?

Whatever you do, leave stingrays alone! Keep in mind that stingrays do not attack unless they are afraid. Even if they are afraid, they will usually swim away.

If you are walking in the water on a beach that has stingrays, you should try to drag your feet when you walk. This will kick up sand and scare away stingrays. You will be less likely to step on one.

Do not panic if you are stung by a stingray. You should call a doctor and put the wound in hot water. Hot water helps fight the venom until you can get to a doctor.

GLOSSARY

camouflages (KA-muh-flah-jez) Hides by using its surroundings.

cartilage (KAHR-tuh-lij) The bendable matter from which people's nose and ears are made.

defense (dih-FENS) Something a living thing does that helps keep it safe.

electrical charges (ih-LEK-trih-kul CHAHRJ-ez) Power that can produce light, heat, or movement.

gills (GILZ) Organs, or body parts, that fish use for breathing.

injects (in-JEKTS) Forces something into the body.

mate (MAYT) When male and female animals make babies.

organs (OR-genz) Parts inside the body that do a job.

predators (PREH-duh-terz) Animals that kill other animals for food.

prey (PRAY) An animal that is eaten by other animals for food.

species (SPEE-sheez) One kind of living thing. All people are one species.

spines (SPYNZ) Hard, pointed edges of a stingray's tail that are often called stingers.

stingers (STING-erz) Sharp objects on an animal's body that can hurt other animals and force venom into their body.

tropical (TRAH-puh-kul) Having to do with the warm parts of Earth.

venom (VEH-num) A poison passed by one animal into another through a bite or a sting.

INDEX

WEB SITES

Due to the changing nature of Internet links, PowerKids Press has developed an online list of Web sites related to the subject of this book. This site is updated regularly. Please use this link to access the list:
www.powerkidslinks.com/poi/sting/